MAGICAL ADVENTURES WITH EMILY AND LIAM

33 fantastic stories for children

James Miller

Copyright © 2023 James Miller

All rights reserved

The characters and events portrayed in this book are fictitious. Any similarity to real persons, living or dead, is coincidental and not intended by the author.

No part of this book may be reproduced, or stored in a retrieval system, or transmitted in any form or by any means, electronic, mechanical, photocopying, recording, or otherwise, without express written permission of the publisher.

This book is a translation of the original German edition.

ISBN: 9798864326206

I dedicate this book to all those who told me it was not possible, but most of all I dedicate it to all those who helped me make it possible.

„Nothing is impossible as long as you believe in it."
J. J.

CONTENTS

Title Page
Copyright
Dedication
Introduction — 3
EMILY'S SPECIAL CAKE CREATION — 4
THE SHOOTING STAR MISSION — 6
THE STOLEN CUP — 8
THE LABYRINTH — 10
THE SECRET GARDEN — 12
THE DISCOVERY — 14
THE TREASURE OF CAPTAIN JOHN — 16
EMILY AND LIAM ON A VOYAGE OF DISCOVERY IN THE RAINFOREST — 18
THE MAGIC GARDEN — 20
JOURNEY INTO THE UNKNOWN — 22
THE GOLDEN TREE — 24
THE FAMILY OUTING — 26
THE SECRET OF THE OLD HOUSE — 28
THE MYSTERIOUS AMULET — 30
THE ADVENTURE IN THE AUTUMN FOREST — 32
AN ANIMAL ADVENTURE — 34

A SPECIAL WINTER DAY	36
The Pirate Island	38
THE TIME TRAVEL TO THE MIDDLE AGES	40
THE MAGIC singing	42
THE MAGIC OF WRITING	44
THE MYSTERIOUS TREASURE	46
THE MAGIC MUSHROOM	48
EMILY AND LIAM ON A MISSION IN SPACE	50
THE LOST PUPPY	52
LIAM'S PIRATE ADVENTURES	54
ANOTHER DOG?	56
AS TREASURE HUNTER IN EGYPT	58
AN UNEXPECTED RAINY DAY	60
THE ENCHANTED FOREST	62
THE AUTUMN WALK	64
THE SECRET CLUB	66
EMMA'S DREAM	68
A SUMMER DAY AT THE LAKE	70
QUIZ - 33 QUESTIONS FOR VERY INTERESTED EXPLORERS & DISCOVERERS	72
QUIZ - SOLUTION	76

Dear parents, dear readers, dear children,

it is my heartfelt pleasure that you can hold the adventures of Hold Emily and Liam in your hands!

I don't want to take up your precious time, because the many adventures that are waiting for you on the coming pages are ready to be experienced...

... So I'll keep it short, it *would help me* and my work as an author if I would get an honest feedback from you after you finished the book in the form of a review on Amazon (duration approx. 5min).

Your review helps other potential readers make an informed decision and give me an idea of how my short stories & illustrations are reaching your children.

Your feedback is therefore not only for me, but also for **for other parents** an enormous help.

I hope your children will enjoy this book & I wish you a lot of fun from the bottom of my heart!

Thank you and let's go on an adventure

James Miller

INTRODUCTION

Welcome to a world of adventure, friendship and fantasy! In this book you will meet the twins Emily and Liam, two children who have countless adventures. Emily is a curious and adventurous girl who has a special connection with nature and animals. Liam, on the other hand, is a brave and athletic boy who loves to play outside and dreams of superheroes and adventures. Together they experience unforgettable adventures and learn important lessons about friendship, cohesion and the value of courage and perseverance.

In this book you will find 33 short stories that Emily and Liam experience as main characters. Each story is unique and tells of new adventures, challenges, and friends that Emily and Liam meet on their travels. Whether they're searching for a lost animal, solving a mystery, or battling nasty villains, you'll have plenty to laugh about, learn about, and discover in these stories.

Join Emily and Liam on their travels through the land of fantasy and be enchanted by their adventures!

EMILY'S SPECIAL CAKE CREATION

Emily has always been an avid amateur baker. When she wasn't playing outside with Liam or doing homework, she loved to spend her time in the kitchen experimenting with different ingredients and recipes. One day, Emily wanted to try something really special. She had an idea for a cake that would not only taste good, but also look great: a rainbow cake!

Liam helped Emily with the shopping and then with preparing the ingredients. Together they mixed the batter, divided it into six bowls, and colored each bowl a different color. Then they took turns pouring small amounts of the batter into a cake pan and putting it in the oven. After half an hour, the cake was done. Emily and Liam took it out of the oven and let it cool. Then the hard part began - cutting the cake into six layers and filling each layer with a different buttercream. It wasn't easy, but Emily and Liam worked together and finally made it.

When the cake was ready, it looked beautiful: six layers in the colors of the rainbow. Emily and Liam were proud of their creation and couldn't wait to taste the cake. They cut off a piece and ate it together. The cake tasted fantastic and was a real eye-catcher. Emily and Liam were happy to have this special baking experience together and decided to try many more exciting recipes.

THE SHOOTING STAR MISSION

Emily and Liam were sitting on the roof of their house watching the night sky. It was a clear night and the stars twinkled brightly in the sky. They had already discovered many constellations, but tonight they had a very special mission: they wanted to see a shooting star and make a wish.
"Do you see anything yet, Liam?" asked Emily excitedly.
"Not yet," Liam replied, "But we have to be patient."
They sat in silence for a while, watching the sky. Suddenly they saw a shooting star that passed quickly in the sky.
"There, did you see her?" exclaimed Emily.
"Yes, I saw them!" replied Liam.
They closed their eyes and both made a wish. Emily wished that her parents would always be happy, and Liam wished that he would become a great explorer someday.
"I hope our wishes come true," Emily said softly. "I believe it will," Liam replied.
They sat there for a while watching the night sky before finally going back into the house.
The next day, they told their friends about the shooting star mission. Emily and Liam wondered if they would ever know if their wishes had come true.

THE STOLEN CUP

Emily and Liam were in a soccer club and were training hard for their next game. They were both very excited and eager to win. The game took place at the weekend and Emily and Liam's team played very well. At the end of the game they had won 2:1 and got a huge cup as a prize.

Emily and Liam were overjoyed and took the cup home to show their parents. But the next day they noticed that the cup had disappeared.

They searched all over the house and asked their parents if they had seen the cup, but no one could help. Emily and Liam were very worried and sad. They decided to ask their friends if they had seen anything.

One of their friends told them that he had seen a suspicious man hanging around near their house the night before. Emily and Liam decided to look for the man and find the trophy.

They watched the man go into a house nearby. Emily and Liam decided to lie in wait until the man left the house again.

Later, when the man had left, they carefully entered the house and set out to find the stolen cup. After a long search, they finally found the huge trophy in an old, wooden cupboard.

Emily and Liam brought the cup back to the club and told their story. Everyone was proud of them and thankful that they had brought the cup back.

THE LABYRINTH

One sunny day Emily and Liam decided to walk through the forest. They saw many animals and plants and had a lot of fun. But when they came to a clearing, they noticed a powerful wizard.
The wizard took them to another world, full of magical creatures and talking animals. A rabbit explained to them that they had landed in the enchanted forest and that only a powerful fairy could lift the spell.
Emily and Liam were determined to return to their own world. The rabbit took them to the fairy who lived in a castle. The fairy heard their story and said that she would help them, but first they had to fulfill a difficult task.
The fairy asked them to get a magic crystal from a maze. Emily and Liam received a map and set out. In the maze they met poisonous spiders, giant snakes and other dangerous creatures, but they fought their way bravely and finally found the crystal.
Back at the fairy, she lifted the spell and they returned to their world.
Emily and Liam were relieved and happy.
They knew they had made an incredible journey in the enchanted forest and were grateful for the help of the friendly animals and the powerful fairy.

THE SECRET GARDEN

Emily and Liam were in the garden playing hide and seek. Emily had found a great hiding place - a small garden surrounded by bushes and trees. Liam could not find her anywhere.

As Emily hid, she spotted a small door at the end of the garden. She opened it and found herself in a beautiful secret garden. There were flowers in all colors and a small bridge that led over a stream, on which the colorful surroundings were reflected.

Emily could hardly believe her luck and called Liam over to tell him about her find. Together they explored the secret garden and then played hide and seek, with the garden becoming their new main hiding place.

Emily and Liam often visited the garden to play and relax. They found out that the garden used to belong to an old lady and had not been maintained for years.

One day they decided to spruce up the garden. They planted new shrubs and colorful flowers.

The secret garden became their new favorite place and they felt like real gardeners.

When they were done, Emily and Liam invited their friends to show them the garden. The friends were thrilled and said that they had never seen such a beautiful garden.

Emily and Liam were proud of their work and thought it was wonderful that they had revived the secret garden.

THE DISCOVERY

Emily and Liam had already experienced many adventures together. But this time it was going to be something very special. They were with their family in a faraway country where everything was different from at home. The streets were full of sounds and smells they had never heard or smelled before.

One day, Emily and Liam decided to go exploring on their own. They wanted to get to know the country and its people better. They wandered through the streets, observed the people doing their daily tasks, and kept discovering new things.

Suddenly they heard a loud music and followed the sound. They came to a square where a colorful group of people were dancing and singing. Emily and Liam danced along and had a lot of fun.

Then they saw a woman selling beautiful jewelry. Emily and Liam were fascinated and bought a bracelet each. The woman spoke a language they didn't understand, but they understood the kindness in her smile.

When it was time to return, Emily and Liam were full of impressions and experiences. They had seen and learned so much that they now understood the country and its culture better. It was an unforgettable adventure that had shown them how wonderful and diverse our world is.

THE TREASURE OF CAPTAIN JOHN

Emily and Liam were out in the forest having fun exploring and discovering. Suddenly they saw an old, rusty chest. They opened it and inside they found a map and a Letter. The letter was from a man named Captain John who had buried a treasure in this forest many years ago. The map showed the way to the treasure.

Emily and Liam were excited and decided to look for the treasure. They followed the map and wandered through the forest. Finally, they came to a river and saw an island in the middle. They knew that the treasure must be hidden on this island.

The two children built a raft and paddled to the island. They searched and searched, but they found nothing. Finally, Emily almost gave up and said, "I think we'll never find the treasure." But Liam didn't give up and said, "We have the map, we'll find it!"

Then Liam saw an old oak tree and remembered the letter from Captain John saying that the treasure was buried under the old oak tree. They dug and dug and finally they found a chest. They opened it and inside was gold, silver and precious stones! They decided to share the gold and treasure with others so that everyone could be happy. They went home and shared their discovery with their family and friends. From that day on, Emily and Liam were not only two happy siblings, but also the ones who found the treasure in the forest.

EMILY AND LIAM ON A VOYAGE OF DISCOVERY IN THE RAINFOREST

Today, when the two siblings had snuggled tiredly under their warm blankets, their mother sat down on Liam's bed and began to read them a story, "Journey into the realm of the rainforest", as she often does. As soon as their mother started reading, Emily's and Liam's eyes became heavy and they sank into their dreams. When they woke up again, they were no longer lying in their cozy beds, but on soft, warm forest floor. To the left and right of them it rustled and cracked. Slowly, the two stood up and looked around. What is this place?" asked Liam. Emily looked at Liam: "I don't know, but let's find out!". The two of them started walking and made their way through the dense undergrowth. After a while, there was a very loud rustling sound next to Emily. "What's that Liam?" she asked. The rustling got louder and suddenly something came jumping out of the nearby bush, a brown monkey. The two jumped back in fright, but the monkey was harmless and gentle. He made it clear to them that they should follow him. Wandering behind the monkey, they crossed large parts of the rainforest and finally arrived at a gigantic waterfall. According to legend, once you have drunk a sip of the water, you will stay young forever," Emily told them. The two approached the waterfall, but before they reached it, their mother stopped reading and closed the book with the story. Sleep well, you two, and have sweet dreams."

THE MAGIC GARDEN

Emily and Liam were inseparable and loved to play outside. One day they came across a hidden garden near their house. The garden was full of colorful flowers and tall trees, and in the middle enthroned an enchanted tree house.
Curious, they decided to explore the tree house and found an old magic wand.
When they picked it up, the garden suddenly shone with bright colors. They could hardly believe their eyes, because magical creatures like unicorns, fairies and dwarves suddenly appeared in the garden.
A unicorn kindly greeted Emily and Liam and explained that they were chosen to protect the garden.
In return, they would always find refuge in the garden when they were in need.
Emily and Liam accepted this important task and spent the rest of the day exploring the garden and making friends with the magical creatures.
They promised to always watch over the garden and protect it.
From now on, they often visited the garden and lovingly cared for the animals and plants.
The garden became their secret and a place full of friendship and peace.

JOURNEY INTO THE UNKNOWN

It was a sunny day in summer when Emily and Liam decided to take a trip into the unknown. They packed their backpacks full of provisions, wore comfortable shoes and started their journey. Their destination was a small island that they had heard seemed to have never been visited by humans. The journey began with a long walk through the forest. Emily and Liam kept a lookout for wild animals and gathered berries and mushrooms. As the sun slowly set, they reached the beach. They spotted a small boat moored on the shore and decided to use it to reach the island. It was an exciting and sometimes frightening journey across the sea. The waves were high and the boat rocked back and forth. But Emily and Liam stuck together and navigated safely to the island. When they arrived, they were overwhelmed by the beauty and peace of the island. It was a small paradise surrounded by turquoise waters and white sandy beaches. They spent the day exploring the island, swimming in the sea and sunbathing on the beach.

As the sun slowly set and darkness fell, they prepared for the return trip. On the boat back on the way to the mainland, they realized that it was an unforgettable adventure. They were proud that they had the courage to travel into the unknown and discover something new.

THE GOLDEN TREE

Liam and Emily were siblings and loved to have adventures together. One day they heard about a mysterious golden tree that supposedly grew on a secluded clearing in the forest. Curious, they decided to find him.

They wandered through dense forests and over high hills until they finally reached the clearing. And there it stood - the golden glowing tree. It radiated a wonderful energy and sparks danced around it like little fairies.

Liam and Emily approached the tree and felt an indescribable magic. When they put their hand on its bark, a secret door opened, leading them to a magical world. There they met friendly beings who accompanied them through fantastic adventures.

They explored dizzying mountains of clouds, dived into glittering underwater worlds and found hidden treasures.

After some time, they had to say goodbye and return. The golden tree closed its door, but the memories of the wonderful experiences would always remain in their hearts.

Liam and Emily returned as brave adventurers, ready for new stories and knowing that there are always magical places and friends waiting for them.

THE FAMILY OUTING

Emily and Liam were full of anticipation for their family trip. This time they were off to the mountains for an exciting hike. With hiking boots on their feet they set off on their way. The climb was exhausting, but the view was incredible. They admired nature and felt free and happy.

Once they reached the top, they took a break and enjoyed a picnic with a view of the mountains. This special moment with the family made them grateful and happy.

On the way back, they decided to take a shortcut, but they got lost in the dense forest. The family was worried and at a loss. But then Emily had an idea!

She asked her father for the map he was carrying, in which all the roads in the area were marked.

Together they looked at the map and tried to find their way. With their combined efforts, the family finally managed to find the right way. The relief was great when they finally found their way back to the car.

This trip was one of the best they had ever experienced. Emily and Liam were proud of themselves and their family, who had overcome this challenge together. They recognized the importance of cohesion and support in difficult situations. It was an unforgettable adventure that they would carry in their hearts for a long time.

THE SECRET OF THE OLD HOUSE

Emily and Liam were on their way home from school when they saw an old house at the end of the street. It looked abandoned and mysterious. They decided to explore it. Cautiously they climbed over the fence and crept around the house. Suddenly they heard a noise and became nervous. They looked around but couldn't see anything suspicious.

Bravely, they entered the house, which was full of dust and faded colors. The stairs led them to a locked room. Curious, they tried to open it. Emily used a hairpin as a tool, which she had previously found on the living room sofa and finally the lock popped open.

They entered the room. It was a beautifully furnished bedroom with red velvet curtains in front of the windows. In the middle of the room was a large blue bed, on which they discovered an old diary. It belonged to a woman who had lived here. Emily and Liam were fascinated by the stories they read in the diary.

They also learned that the woman was still alive and in a nursing home.

They visited her and listened intently. After the old woman had finished telling the story and Emily and Liam had said goodbye, they set off for home.

Once home, Emily and Liam agreed that they would carry the secret of the house in their hearts forever.

THE MYSTERIOUS AMULET

Emily and Liam were excited. In an antique store, they discovered an old, magical amulet. The shopkeeper told them that it came from the land of fantasy and had magic powers.

At first they thought he was just kidding, but they still decided to buy the amulet and try it out.

As they wore it around their necks, something incredible happened - they were pulled into another world.

There were dragons, unicorns and elves there. Emily and Liam were overwhelmed and began to explore the new world. The amulet gave them magical abilities that made their dreams come true.

But they also learned that the fantasy world was in danger. An evil wizard had stolen all the magic.

Determined, Emily and Liam decided to defeat the wizard. Together with elves and unicorns they fought against him.

With their imagination and the magic amulet, they managed to defeat the wizard and bring back the magic.

Back in their own world, they knew they would always believe in the power of imagination and courage.

They had learned that with imagination and determination you can achieve great things.

THE ADVENTURE IN THE AUTUMN FOREST

Emily and Liam had been walking in the autumn forest when they suddenly heard a chirping sound. They followed the sound and came to a large stone that was under the red leafy canopy stood among all the trees. On it they saw a beautiful bird that greeted them with its song and as they approached it flew into the forest.

Emily and Liam were fascinated by the bird and decided to follow it. They went deeper into the forest and came to a lake. There they saw many colorful leaves that had fallen from the tree.

Suddenly it became very windy and the leaves swirled around them. Emily and Liam started laughing and dancing among the falling leaves. They were having so much fun that they almost forgot to follow the bird.

As they walked along, they noticed that the forest was getting darker and the bird could no longer be heard. They began to be a little afraid when suddenly a deer ran by. The deer seemed to be showing them something, so they followed it. It led them to a cave where they found a small squirrel gathering its supplies for the winter.

Emily and Liam helped the squirrel gather his supplies and then began to walk back.

Emily and Liam decided that they should visit the Autumn Forest more often for more adventures and went home.

AN ANIMAL ADVENTURE

It was a sunny day at the zoo. Emily and Liam discovered the different animals and were especially fascinated by the elephants and monkeys. But at the lion enclosure, they noticed that something was wrong. A lion was restless
and ran in circles.
They asked the keeper what was going on. The lion missed his runaway comrade.
Emily and Liam asked the keeper for permission to help with the search. Skeptical at first, he eventually let them go.
Together they combed the zoo and quickly found the lion's track.
He had hidden in the nearby forest. But the lion was injured and could not walk. The children called the vet and helped him wrap the lion's wound with a bandage.
When the lion was healthy again after a few weeks, he returned to his comrade.
Emily and Liam were proud of their rescue.
The zoo thanked them and presented them with a medal. They told everyone about this adventure. They knew that together they could master any adventure.

A SPECIAL WINTER DAY

Emily and Liam couldn't wait to visit the winter market. There were lights and music everywhere, and it smelled like roasted almonds and gingerbread. They strolled along the booths and sampled all the different treats.

Suddenly, Emily saw a booth with handicrafts and decided to buy a homemade Christmas gift for her mother. When she turned around to find Liam, he had disappeared.

She searched the whole market but could not find him anywhere. Emily decided to leave the market and go home to inform her parents. But when she stepped out of the market, she saw Liam standing at the end of the street, waving.

He had found a booth where you could get makeup and he had dressed up as a snowman.

Emily laughed and ran over to him before hugging him.

They told each other about all the wonderful things they had seen at the market and enjoyed the rest of the day together.

That evening, when they were back home, they told their parents about their special winter day and they rejoiced in the memories they had made together. Emily and Liam knew that this would be a day they would remember for a long time.

THE PIRATE ISLAND

It was a clear night when Emily woke up from an exciting dream as a pirate. She felt like she was on a ship and still had the smell of the salty sea water in her nose. Liam was sitting over his sister anxiously on his bed. "What's wrong, Emily?" he asked. "I had an exciting pirate dream," she told him excitedly. Liam laughed. "Pirates only exist in movies and books." But Emily was determined to make her dream come true.

The next day they set off for the coast. Emily had found a map that led to an island where pirates supposedly lived. The journey was hard, but Emily and Liam fought their way through the jungle and over mountains.

Finally they reached the coast and found an abandoned ship. They declared it their pirate ship and set sail.

Eventually they discovered the island, but they were just kids in disguise. Emily and Liam joined them and had a great time. They sailed, explored the island, and fought made-up enemies. They learned that they can accomplish anything if they stick together and are brave. Emily and Liam were grateful for this experience and kept it in their hearts forever.

THE TIME TRAVEL TO THE MIDDLE AGES

Emily and Liam were excited when they found a strange object in their backyard that looked like an old clock. Little did they know that it was a magical clock that allowed them to travel through time.

Suddenly, the garden around them went dark, and they felt themselves catapulted through space and time. When they opened their eyes, they found themselves in a medieval city.

The children were fascinated by the knights in their shining armor and the horses galloping along the streets.

Emily and Liam met a friendly family who helped them find their way around town. They learned how to grow vegetables, bake bread, and even learn archery. The children spent their days discovering life in the Middle Ages and making new friends.

But soon they found out that there were also dangers. A group of bandits wanted to attack the town and steal the supplies. Emily and Liam decided to help by warning the guards and supporting their new friends. With their help, they managed to defend the town and drive away the bandits.

At the end of the day, the children found themselves in their parents' garden again. They didn't know if they had dreamed or if it had really happened. But they knew that they had a wonderful time in the Middle Ages and that they would always remember the friendships they had made.

THE MAGIC SINGING

Emily and Liam were full of anticipation for the concert they were about to attend. But when the music started to play, they immediately noticed that something unusual was happening. The sounds seemed to come from another world and to cast a magical spell over her. The music enveloped her like an invisible mist and made her float while reality blurred around her. Suddenly, a singer appeared on stage and began to sing. Her voice was so magical that Emily and Liam thought they were surrounded by angels. Emily and Liam were enchanted and forgot everything around them. They were alone with the singer and her music. When the song ended, the singer disappeared without a trace and the world returned.

Emily and Liam were still filled with music and had a desire to find the singer. They inquired with people, but
no one knew where she was.

But Emily and Liam were not discouraged. They searched the city, the countryside, and even hidden places until they finally arrived at a secluded house. They knocked on the door and an old lady opened. It was the singer, who was very happy to see the unexpected guests. Emily and Liam were amazed and in awe. They spent a lot of time with the singer and had great conversations about her music. So they left the house feeling grateful to have met such a great person.

THE MAGIC OF WRITING

Emily and Liam were in the park as usual on the weekend, playing happily, when by chance they met your grandfather. He had a gray beard and was wearing a beautiful blue Coat. "Kids, are you up for a little adventure?" their grandfather asked. Emily and Liam looked at each other and nodded excitedly.

He opened his coat pocket and took out an old leather-bound book. On the cover was a golden feather.

"This book is the magic book of writing," he said. "If you write in it, you can bring your thoughts and ideas to life." Emily and Liam looked at each other and thought about what they could write. Liam decided to write about a flying dragon, while Emily wrote about a talking cat. Then something magical happened.

A flying dragon appeared in the sky and flew in circles over the park, while a talking cat approached Emily and Liam and gave them a friendly greeting.

"That's the magic of writing," her grandfather said. "With this book, you can create anything you can imagine." Emily and Liam could hardly believe their luck when their grandfather suddenly told them that they could keep the book for themselves. They thanked their grandfather and promised to keep the magic book of writing well and use it only for good purposes.

THE MYSTERIOUS TREASURE

Emily and Liam had been searching for the mysterious treasure near the hidden cave for a long time. When they finally found the cave, they discovered a huge rock, that blocked the entrance. They tried to move the rock, but it was much too difficult for them. Suddenly they heard a noise and saw a man coming towards them.
"What are you doing here?" the man asked.
"We're looking for the treasure in the cave," Emily replied.
The old man explained that he was an experienced treasure hunter and knew a lot about caves. He offered to help them move the rock and find the treasure in exchange for helping him with some tasks. Emily and Liam agreed and helped the old man repair his house and tend his vegetable garden. After they finished the tasks, the man helped them move the rock in front of the cave entrance. Once inside the cave, they found a secret door that led to a room full of gold and jewels. Emily and Liam were overwhelmed and could hardly believe their luck.
The old man said that they could share the treasure, which made Emily and Liam incredibly happy.
However, they were clear that they wanted to use their share for something meaningful and so they donated everything except two beautiful sparkling diamonds, which they kept as a memento, to a good cause.

THE MAGIC MUSHROOM

Emily and Liam loved to have adventures and when they heard about an enchanted forest nearby, they were thrilled. The forest was unlike anything they had ever seen. The trees seemed to be alive and the leaves were painted in bright colors. As they looked around, they suddenly heard a soft whisper and discovered a little elf named Alva. She explained to the children that they could only leave the enchanted forest if they completed a difficult task. Emily and Liam would have to find a rare mushroom that could only grow in complete darkness.

Emily and Liam set off and fought their way through the dense forest. Finally, they came to a cave where it was pitch black. But when they turned on their flashlights, they saw the rare mushroom right in front of them. They picked the mushroom and when they came out of the cave, the forest magically began to glow. They returned to Alva and gave her the mushroom.

Alva thanked them and explained that after they had mastered this difficult task, they could leave this enchanted place. Emily and Liam made their way back, grateful for having had such an incredible adventure and for all the valuable experiences they had had.

EMILY AND LIAM ON A MISSION IN SPACE

Emily and Liam were astronauts on their first space mission. They were on their way to a distant planet to study it for a school project. But suddenly their spaceship got caught in an asteroid shower and was severely damaged. Emily and Liam had to act quickly to save their lives. They put on their spacesuits and headed into space to repair the damage
to the spaceship.
The repair was more difficult than expected, and they had to protect themselves against the dangers of space, such as cold and, of course, the meteorites that shot past them. After successfully repairing the spaceship, they continued their mission and landed on the planet. There they discovered an amazing world full of new creatures, like the fluffy wispies which were furry creatures with iridescent wings and spread rainbow dust. But they also encountered many dangers, but they did not give up and overcame every challenge they encountered on their mission. When they finally returned to Earth, they were heroes and celebrated by the whole world. Emily and Liam were proud to have been part of such an important mission and couldn't wait to set off on new adventures in space.

THE LOST PUPPY

Emily and Liam were on their way to the park when they spotted a little puppy on the street. He was dirty and had matted fur, so Emily and Liam decided to help him. They took the puppy home and gave him a bath. The puppy was so grateful that he cuddled with Emily and Liam all evening. They decided to keep him and named him Charlie.

Charlie was a bright and incredibly sweet puppy and loved to run around and play. One day Emily and Liam left the door open and Charlie ran away. Emily and Liam were worried and looked everywhere for him, but he was nowhere to be found.

They decided to distribute flyers in the neighborhood and asked for help in finding Charlie. After a few days, a call finally came. Someone had seen Charlie in a nearby park.

Emily and Liam immediately made their way to the park. They called Charlie's name and looked around. Finally, they heard a bark and followed the sound. They found Charlie jumping up and down happily when he saw them.

Emily and Liam hugged Charlie and took him home. They were relieved to have found him and vowed never to let him out of their sight again. From that day on, Charlie was always by their side and the three of them were inseparable.

LIAM'S PIRATE ADVENTURES

Liam had always dreamed of being a pirate. One night he had a strange dream in which he was sailing on a huge ship and traveling around the world with a pirate crew. But when he woke up, he was disappointed that it had only been a dream.
But the next day, Liam got an invitation to a special event at a nearby museum of science and technology. There was an exhibition there about pirates and their ships. Liam could hardly believe how real the models looked. He was so fascinated by the exhibits that he felt like a pirate.
Suddenly, Liam heard a strange noise and felt the floor move beneath him. He looked around and noticed that the ship in the middle of the room he was standing on began to move. Confused and surprised, he looked around and realized that he was actually on a real pirate ship.
The crew around him laughed and hailed him as the new captain. Liam could hardly believe it, but he had made it - he was finally a pirate! He enjoyed his new role as captain and sailed around the world with his crew.
When Liam woke up, he remembered his dream and smiled. Even though it was just a dream, it felt so real. He felt that he could achieve anything if he only
believed in it.

ANOTHER DOG?

Emily and Liam were still enthralled with their dog Charlie, whom they had taken in some time ago. The two siblings were incredibly fond of Charlie and every day they would go with him Gassie.

One day, however, when they had left the park as usual and were walking back to their home on the pedestrian path, they noticed something beside them.

A brown beautiful dog with a golden necklace. Charlie and the unknown dog understood each other directly and seemed to like each other very much, because they started to play with each other directly.

Emily and Liam looked around but could not find the dog's master anywhere.

In the store next door, they excitedly asked if anyone knew the dog's owner, but they did not.

Not long after, they were no longer three on the way home, but four. Emily and Liam had spontaneously decided to take the new dog, whom they named Tommy, home with them and thus offer him a home.

"Liam, what if Mom says that two dogs is one too many?" said Emily nervously. "She won't, because..." and before he could finish the sentence, her mother opened the front door and greeted all four of them warmly. After Emily briefly told her mother the situation, she and their father agreed to take Tommy in. Emily and Liam were then overjoyed that they were now four.

AS TREASURE HUNTER IN EGYPT

Emily and Liam were at school learning about the ancient cultures of the world. They were especially fascinated by the ancient Egyptians and their pyramids. One day they decided to go on a treasure hunt and discover some of the ancient history for yourself.

They found an old map in the library that showed the way to a secret treasure hidden somewhere in the pyramids.

So Emily and Liam started their journey, got on the next plane and flew as fast as possible to the gigantic pyramids.

When they finally arrived at the pyramids after a long flight and a bumpy cab ride, the two made their way into one of the pyramids and followed the map through dark tunnels and narrow passages until they finally reached a chamber filled with gold and jewels.

But before they could do anything, they heard footsteps. A guard of the pyramid had discovered them!

Emily and Liam ran through the hallways trying to lose the guard. They had to use a lot of skill and courage to distract him and finally escape.

When they got back to the library, they could hardly believe their luck. They had actually found a treasure!

But more importantly, they had grown even closer as siblings.

AN UNEXPECTED RAINY DAY

Emily and Liam had been looking forward to the trip to the amusement park for days. But when they finally got there, it suddenly started to rain. Disappointed, they sought shelter under a big tree.

"This is so unfair," Emily muttered, "we were so looking forward to this and now we can't do anything."

"Maybe it will stop raining soon," Liam tried to cheer her up.

But it rained and rained and did not stop.

Finally, they decided to go back to the car.

But on the way they discovered a hall where there were many games and attractions that could be enjoyed even in rainy weather.

Emily and Liam ran inside and spent the rest of the day riding roller coasters, playing can toss, and eating popcorn.

"This was the best rainy day ever," Liam said as they walked back to the car.

"Yeah, right," Emily agreed, "I'm glad we didn't give up."

And so they learned that day that even in bad weather there is always a way to have fun.

THE ENCHANTED FOREST

Emily and Liam loved to play outside in nature. One day they decided to explore the forest on the outskirts of their town. They had played there many times before, but they had never explored the entire forest.

As they went deeper into the forest, they noticed that the environment was slowly changing.

The trees were taller and denser, and it almost seemed as if the forest was enclosing them. They did not know that they had entered an enchanted forest.

Suddenly they heard a voice calling them.

They followed the voice and saw a little fairy floating on a leaf in a stream.

The fairy explained to them that they had landed in the enchanted forest, which had been cursed by an evil wizard.

Emily and Liam were brave enough to help the fairy
break the curse.

Together they searched for the wizard and finally
found him in a cave.

After a hard fight, they were able to defeat the wizard and free the forest.

The fairy thanked Emily and Liam and said goodbye.

The two children happily returned from the forest and told everyone about their adventure.

THE AUTUMN WALK

Emily and Liam loved to walk outside in the fall and collect the colorful leaves. One sunny afternoon, they decided to go to the nearby park to collect their leaf and cone collection to begin.

While walking through the park, they noticed an older man working on a block of wood. Emily and Liam were curious and approached him. The man introduced himself as Mr. Jefferson and explained to the children that he was a sculptor and carved the pieces of wood into figures.

Emily and Liam were fascinated by Mr. Jefferson's work and decided to ask him if he could teach them how to carve. Mr. Jefferson agreed and gave the children a few pieces of wood to start their own carving.

The sun slowly began to set as Emily and Liam finished their carving and headed home. They were proud of their work and looked forward to seeing Mr. Jefferson again on the next fall walk. From that day on, Emily and Liam made it a tradition to take a walk through the park in the fall and visit Mr. Jefferson to improve their carving skills. Autumn had become their favorite time of year because they could not only enjoy the colorful nature, but also improve their creativity and craftsmanship.

THE SECRET CLUB

Emily and Liam were twins and resembled best friends. One day they decided to start a secret club. They wanted to have a secret hideout where they could meet and have adventures.

They searched all over the house for a suitable hiding place and finally found an old shed in the garden. The shed was a bit rusty and had some holes in the roof, but that didn't bother Emily and Liam. They decided to make the shed their clubhouse.

They spent the whole afternoon cleaning and decorating the shed. They even wrote "Secret Club" on the door. Then they planned their first secret mission.

Their mission was to find the fabled magic rose. Emily and Liam set off into the forest looking for clues. They followed a trail of arrows that led them to an old tree stump. There they found a map that showed the way to the magic rose.

They followed the map and finally came across a hidden room under a rock. In the room they found a small mound of earth from which a radiant red rose grew. Emily and Liam were thrilled and could hardly believe their luck, because according to legend, the rose was supposed to make all their wishes come true. After this remarkable find, they celebrated their success and decided to have many more adventures as a secret club.

EMMA'S DREAM

Emma had a dream as she slept soundly one night in her bed next to Liam's - she wanted to be a famous ballet dancer. Ever since she was a little girl, she had worn the ballet shoes and practiced her steps. And her best
Girlfriend Antonia always supported her by sitting in the audience at every performance and cheering her on.
One day there was a big ballet competition in town. Emma and Antonia were so excited that they could hardly sleep. On the day of the competition, Emma felt nervous and insecure, but when she went on stage and the music started, her fear disappeared and she danced as if she were flying.
After the competition was over and all the dancers had shown their performances, it was time for the results. Emma held her breath as the emcee announced, "And first place goes to.... Emma!" She could hardly believe it - she had actually won!
When she got home, the two girls danced around the living room with joy, and Antonia suggested that they have a party to celebrate Emma's victory.
And so it happened - Emma celebrated her victory with her friends and family and finally felt ready to tackle her next goal: getting a spot at the most prestigious ballet school in town. She knew it was a long road, but with persistence and discipline, she would make it.

A SUMMER DAY AT THE LAKE

Emily and Liam had been looking forward to summer for weeks. It was finally here and they spent their days outside in the sun, swimming in the lake and playing on the beach. One day they decided to explore the lake by boat. It was a beautiful day and the water was glistening in the sun. They paddled leisurely along, enjoying the peace and beauty of nature.
Suddenly they heard a loud splash. They looked around and saw that someone had jumped into the water.
It was a girl they did not know. She swam towards them and introduced herself as Lina.
Emily and Liam immediately became friends with her and spent the rest of the day together at the lake.
They played volleyball, built sand castles and ate delicious ice cream. The day went by way too fast and they decided to meet again the next day.
The next day they met again at the lake and spent another beautiful day together.
From then on they met regularly and became good friends.
Summer flew by and before they knew it, it was time to get ready for school again. But Emily and Liam knew they would always have good memories of their summer at the lake and their new friend Lina.

QUIZ - 33 QUESTIONS FOR VERY INTERESTED EXPLORERS & DISCOVERERS

Questions for little explorers

1. How many months are in a year?

2. Which animal in the zoo has a long neck and can grow up to six meters?

3. How many hours are in a day?

4. What color is a ripe banana?

5. How many fingers does a hand have?

6. What color is the sun?

7. Who is the "king" among the animals?

8. How many days are in a week?

9. What is the first letter in the alphabet?

10. Which animal can fly and produce honey?

11. How many colors does a traffic light have?

Questions for great explorers

12. How many minutes are in an hour?

13. What do you call someone who works in a hospital and makes

people well?

14. How many players are on the soccer field per team?

15. How many seasons are there in a year?

16. How many legs does a spider have?

17. What is the name of the capital of Germany?

18. Which is bigger: the sun or the moon?

19. How many days are in a year?

20. How many sides does a triangle have?

21. What do you call someone who writes books?

22. What do you call someone who flies in space?

Questions for real adventurers

23. What is the name of the highest mountain in the world?

24. How many teeth does an adult person normally have?

25. What do you call the day before Christmas?

26. How many letters does the German alphabet have?

27. How many colors does a rainbow have?

28. What do you call a group of sheep?

29. What is the name of the largest continent on earth?

30. What is the name of the largest ocean on earth?

31. How many planets are there in our solar system?

32. What is the largest organ in the human body?

33. Which is the largest country in the world?

Solutions on the coming pages!

QUIZ - SOLUTION

Questions for little explorers

1. A year has 12 months.

2. A giraffe has a long neck and can grow up to six meters.

3. A day has 24 hours.

4. A ripe banana is yellow.

5. One hand has five fingers.

6. The sun appears yellow.

7. This is the lion.

8. A week has seven days.

9. The first letter in the alphabet is the "A".

10. A bee can fly and produce honey.

11. A traffic light has three colors: red, yellow and green.

Questions for great explorers

12. One hour has 60 minutes.

13. A doctor in the hospital makes people well.

14. In soccer, there are 11 players per team on the field.

15. There are four seasons in a year.

16. A spider usually has eight legs.

17. The capital of Germany is Berlin.

18. The sun is bigger than the moon.

19. A year has 365 days (in most cases).

20. A triangle has three sides.

21. Someone who writes books is called an author.

22. Someone who flies in space is called an astronaut.

Questions for real adventurers

23. The highest mountain in the world is called Mount Everest.

24. An adult human normally has 32 teeth.

25. The day before Christmas is called Christmas Eve.

26. The German alphabet has 26 letters.

27. A rainbow has seven colors.

28. A group of sheep is called a flock.

29. The largest continent on earth is called Asia.

30. The largest ocean on earth is called the Pacific Ocean.

31. There are eight planets in our solar system.

32. The largest organ in the human body is the skin.

33. The largest country in the world is Russia.

Dear parents, dear readers, dear children,

I am very pleased that you have come to this page!

I don't want to take up your precious time, for surely there are many more adventures outside of this book waiting for the listening children who are waiting to be experienced...

... Therefore I will be brief, it *would help me* and my work as an author if I would receive an honest feedback from you in the form of a review on Amazon
(duration approx. 5min).

Your review helps other potential readers make an informed decision and give me an idea of how my short stories & illustrations are reaching your children.

Your feedback is therefore not only for me, but also for **for other parents** an enormous help.

I hope your children have enjoyed this book & I thank you from the bottom of my heart for reading.

Thank you for your support
James Miller

Printed in Great Britain
by Amazon